DATA MANIA
Sorting Fur, Feathers, Tails, and Scales

I'm Matt Maticus. I love mathematics! Sorting is an important part of math. Join me on the savanna, and I'll show you how!

by Marcie Aboff

Consultant:
Michele Koomen, PhD
Co-Chair and Assistant Professor of Education
Gustavus Adolphus College
St. Peter, Minnesota

CAPSTONE PRESS
a capstone imprint

First Facts is published by Capstone Press,
151 Good Counsel Drive, P.O. Box 669, Mankato, Minnesota 56002.
www.capstonepub.com

Copyright © 2011 by Capstone Press, a Capstone imprint.
All rights reserved.
No part of this publication may be reproduced in whole or in part, or stored in a retrieval system, or transmitted in any form or by any means, electronic, mechanical, photocopying, recording, or otherwise, without written permission of the publisher. For information regarding permission, write to Capstone Press, 151 Good Counsel Drive, P.O. Box 669, Dept. R, Mankato, Minnesota 56002.
Printed in the United States of America in Melrose Park, Illinois.
032010
005742LKF10

 Books published by Capstone Press are manufactured with paper containing at least 10 percent post-consumer waste.

Library of Congress Cataloging-in-Publication Data
Aboff, Marcie.
  Sorting fur, feathers, tails, and scales / by Marcie Aboff.
    p. cm.—(First facts. data mania)
  Summary: "Uses animals on the African savanna to explore how sorting can help readers organize and understand information"—Provided by publisher.
  Includes bibliographical references and index.
  ISBN 978-1-4296-4526-3 (library binding)
 1. Set theory—Juvenile literature. I. Title. II. Series.

QA248.A235 2011
511.3'22—dc22   2010000553

Editorial Credits
Christopher L. Harbo, editor; Matt Bruning, designer and illustrator; Eric Manske,
      production specialist

Photo Credits
iStockphoto: Eric Isselée, 5 (ostrich), 15, Stanislav Mikhalev, 21, Stilyan Savov, background
      (throughout), Tomasz Zachariasz, 13 (worm)
Shutterstock: Anna Jurkovska, 11 (spots), Arsgera, 11 (solids), Ashley Whitworth, 19
      (giraffe), Birute Vijeikiene, 5 (background), Christian Musat, 7 (giraffe), Daniel Krylov,
      13 (butterfly), Eric Isselée, 5 (zebra, lion, vulture, cheetah, hyena), 9, 11, 13, 15, 17
      (rhino), 19 (leopard), Four Oaks, 9 (wildebeest), Gerrit_de_Vries, 9 (weaver bird), 9
      (warthog), 11, 13, 15, 19, Gilmanshin, 9 (snake), 13, Jason Prince, 5 (elephant), 13, 19,
      Johan Swanepoel, 7 (elephant), 17 (oryx), 19, pandapaw, 11 (giraffe), Reinhold Leitner, 9
      (meerkat), 11, 17, 19, Sara Robinson, 7 (lion), Shebeko, 11 (feathers), thoron, 7 (zebra)

Table of Contents

Savanna Sorting 4

Oh My, Let's Classify! 6

Dare to Compare 12

Breaking Down Categories 14

Venn Diagrams 18

Sorting On and On 20

Glossary 22

Read More 23

Internet Sites 23

Index 24

Savanna Sorting

It's great to be home! The African savanna has hundreds of animals. Just look at all of the elephants, zebras, and lions. So many animals live here, sometimes I lose count!

Luckily, sorting helps me **organize** things into groups. It can also show me how things are the same or different.

organize—to arrange things neatly and in order

Oh My, Let's Classify!

When we sort, groups are **classified** by something they have in common. Classifying helps you arrange things so they are easier to count.

To sort by animal type, we need to get the animals into groups. The giraffes **gather** in one group. The elephants, zebras, and other animals gather in their own groups. Then we can count the animals we sorted into each group.

classify—to put things into groups according to their characteristics

gather—to bring together

Bar Graphs

A bar graph shows the number of animals in each group. This bar graph shows how many zebras, elephants, lions, and giraffes we have. The longer the bar, the more animals there are.

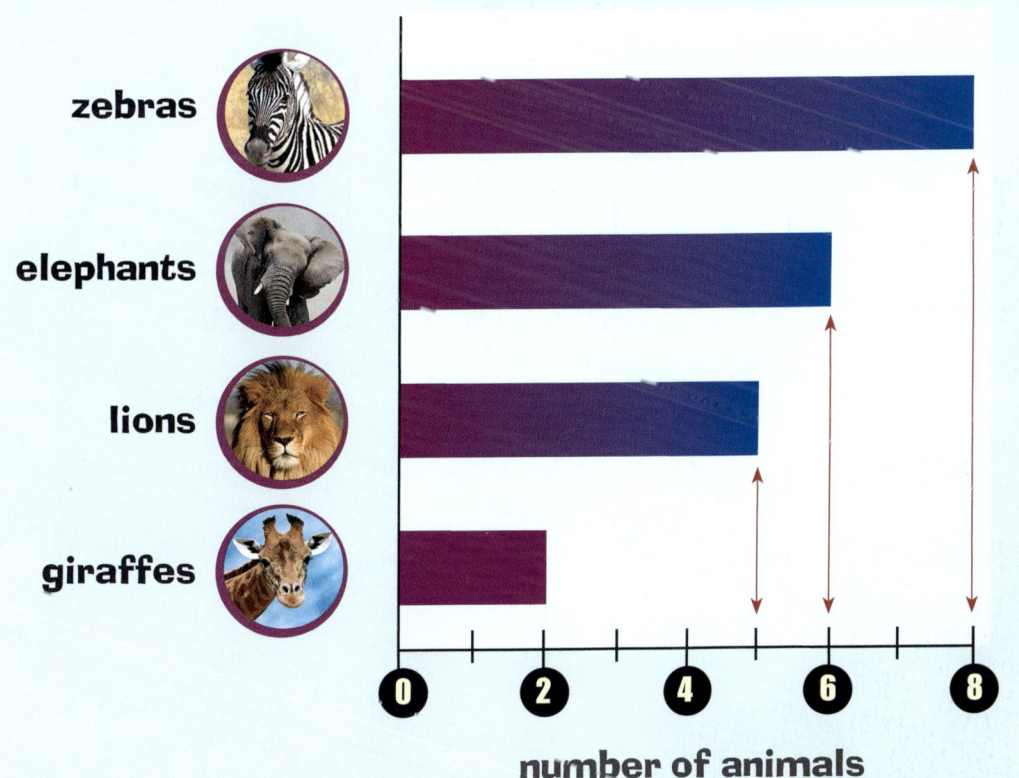

number of animals

Animal type isn't the only way to classify groups on the savanna. My home has large wildebeests and tiny birds. Let's sort the animals by size. The birds and snakes gather in the small group. The meerkats and warthogs are in the medium group. The wildebeests and zebras make up the large group.

Grouping by Size

small animals   medium animals   large animals

Classifying also helps you focus on one detail and forget about others. Animal fur can be spotted or plain. Some animals have feathers. If I sort by body covering, do I need to know the size of the animals? No, only their body covering is needed to sort them.

| spots | plain | feathers |

Important Decisions

How we sort things decides what groups we have. Say you want to sort animals that climb trees. To do this, you don't need to know if they have horns. You only need to find out if they climb trees. Their other features don't matter.

Dare to Compare

Animals move in different ways. Sorting can help us **compare** how they move. When you compare, you find out how things are the same or different.

I picked seven animals and sorted them into groups by how they move. Compare the three groups. Do more animals walk, crawl, or fly?

compare—to judge one thing against another and note the similarities and differences

Comparing Movement

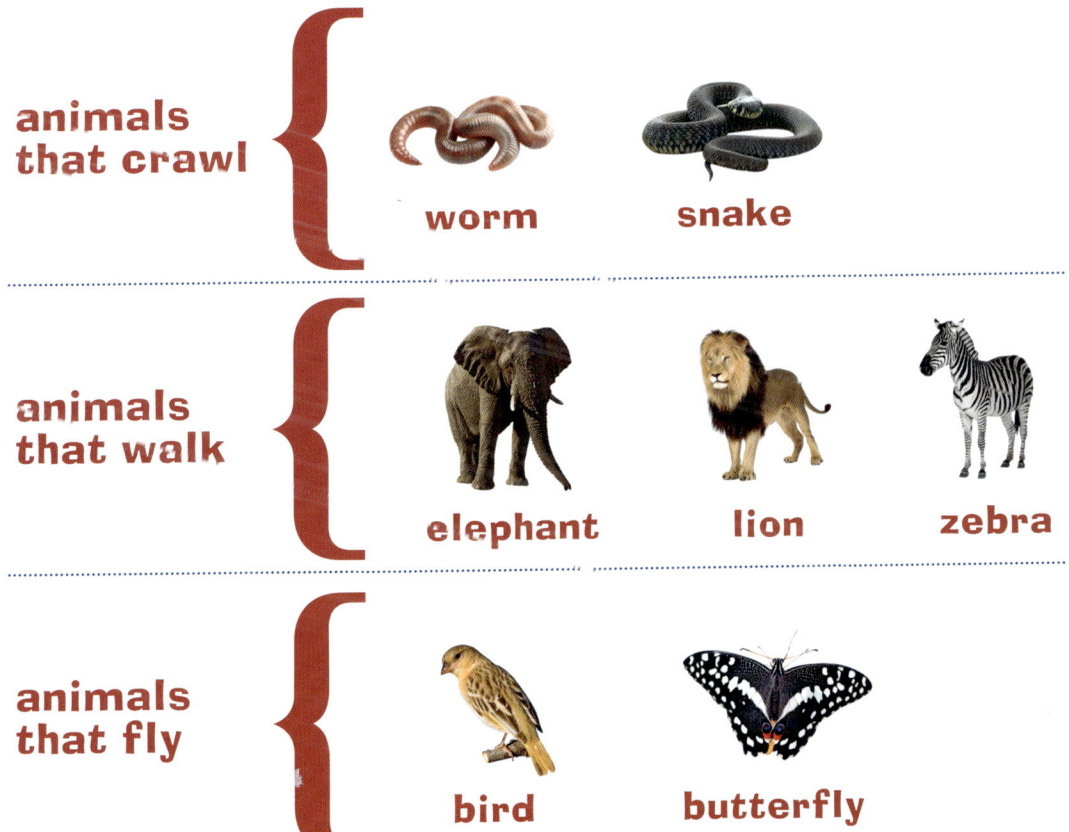

Breaking Down Categories

When you sort, you can put animals into **categories**. Categories help you break a larger group into smaller groups.

We can classify all the birds as one group of animals. But not all birds fly. We can sort the birds into one group that flies and another group that doesn't fly.

category—a class or group of things that has something in common

Let's use categories in a larger group. Which animals have curved horns and which have straight horns? First I sort the horned animals into one group. Then I sort them into groups with straight and curved horns. Using categories helped me find the information I need.

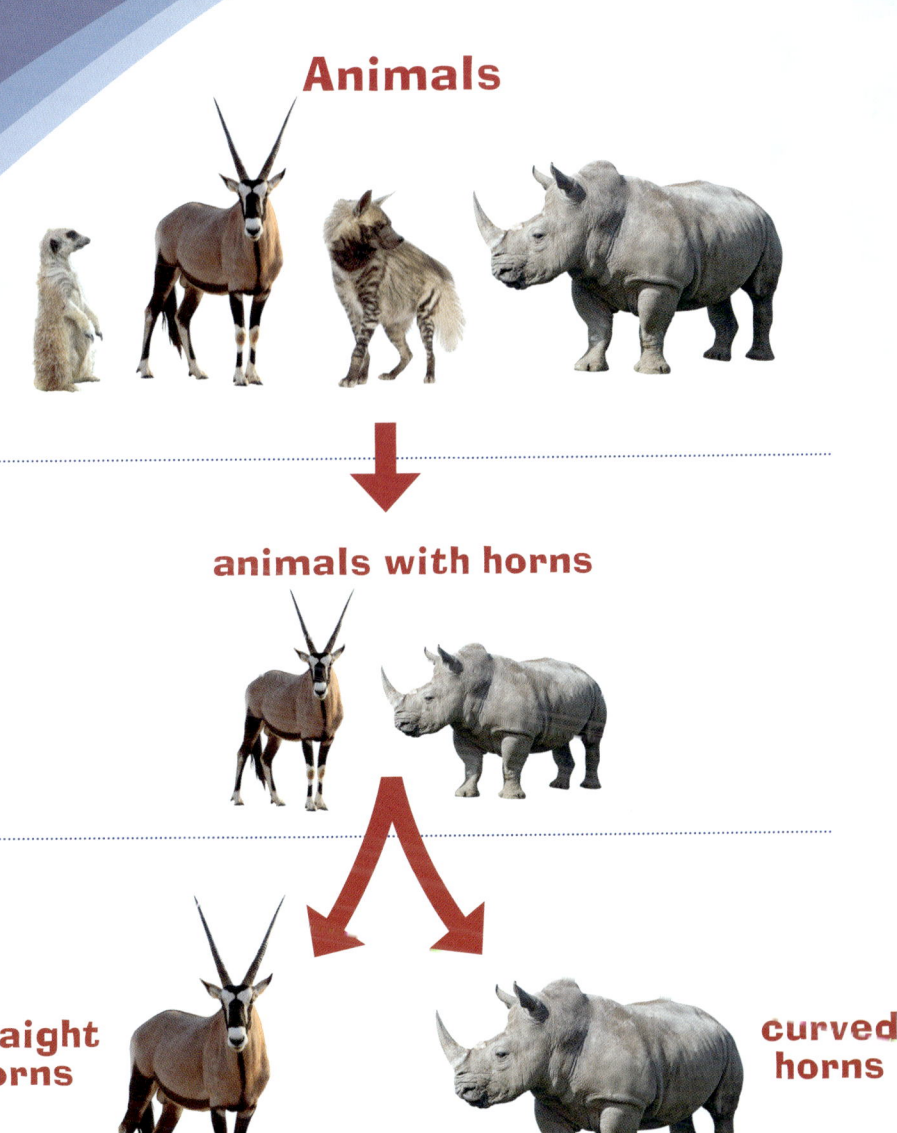

Venn Diagrams

Chomp, crunch, munch. Animals love to eat! Some animals eat only plants. Others just eat meat. Another group of animals eats meat and plants.

A Venn diagram uses circles to sort animals by how they eat. The top circle has animals that eat plants. The bottom circle shows animals that eat meat. See how the circles **overlap**? That part shows animals that eat both plants and meat.

overlap—the part of two groups that has something in common

Sorting On and On

Life on the savanna is always changing. In a few days, lion cubs will be born. Sorting will come in handy when I want to classify the young from the old. Or maybe I'll sort the males from the females. Either way, sorting helps me organize the animals on the savanna.

Glossary

category (KAT-uh-gor-ee)—a class or group of things that has something in common

classify (KLASS-uh-fye)—to put things into groups according to their characteristics

compare (kuhm-PAIR)—to judge one thing against another and note the similarities and differences

gather (GATH-ur)—to bring together in one group

organize (OR-guh-nize)—to arrange things neatly and in order

overlap (oh-vur-LAP)—the part of two groups that has something in common

Read More

Aboff, Marcie. *If You Were a Set.* Math Fun. Minneapolis: Picture Window Books, 2009.

Mariconda, Barbara. *Sort it Out!* Mount Pleasant, S.C.: Sylvan Dell Publishing, 2008.

Ribke, Simone T. *Grouping at the Dog Show.* Rookie Read-About Math. New York: Children's Press, 2006.

Internet Sites

FactHound offers a safe, fun way to find Internet sites related to this book. All of the sites on FactHound have been researched by our staff.

Here's all you do:

Visit *www.facthound.com*

FactHound will fetch the best sites for you!

Index

bar graphs, 7

categories, 14, 16
classifying, 6, 8, 10, 14, 20
comparing, 12
counting, 4, 5, 6

decisions, 11
details, 10
differences, 4, 12

features, 11

gathering, 6, 8
groups, 4, 6, 7, 8, 11, 12, 14, 16, 18

information, 16

organizing, 4, 20

similarities, 4, 12

Venn diagrams, 18

Sorting fur, feathers, tails, and scales